USDA

United States
Department of
Agriculture

Forest Service

Pacific Northwest
Research Station

General Technical
Report
PNW-GTR-862

October 2012

Adaptations to Climate Change: Colville and Okanogan-Wenatchee National Forests

William L. Gaines, David W. Peterson, Cameron A. Thomas, and Richy J. Harrod

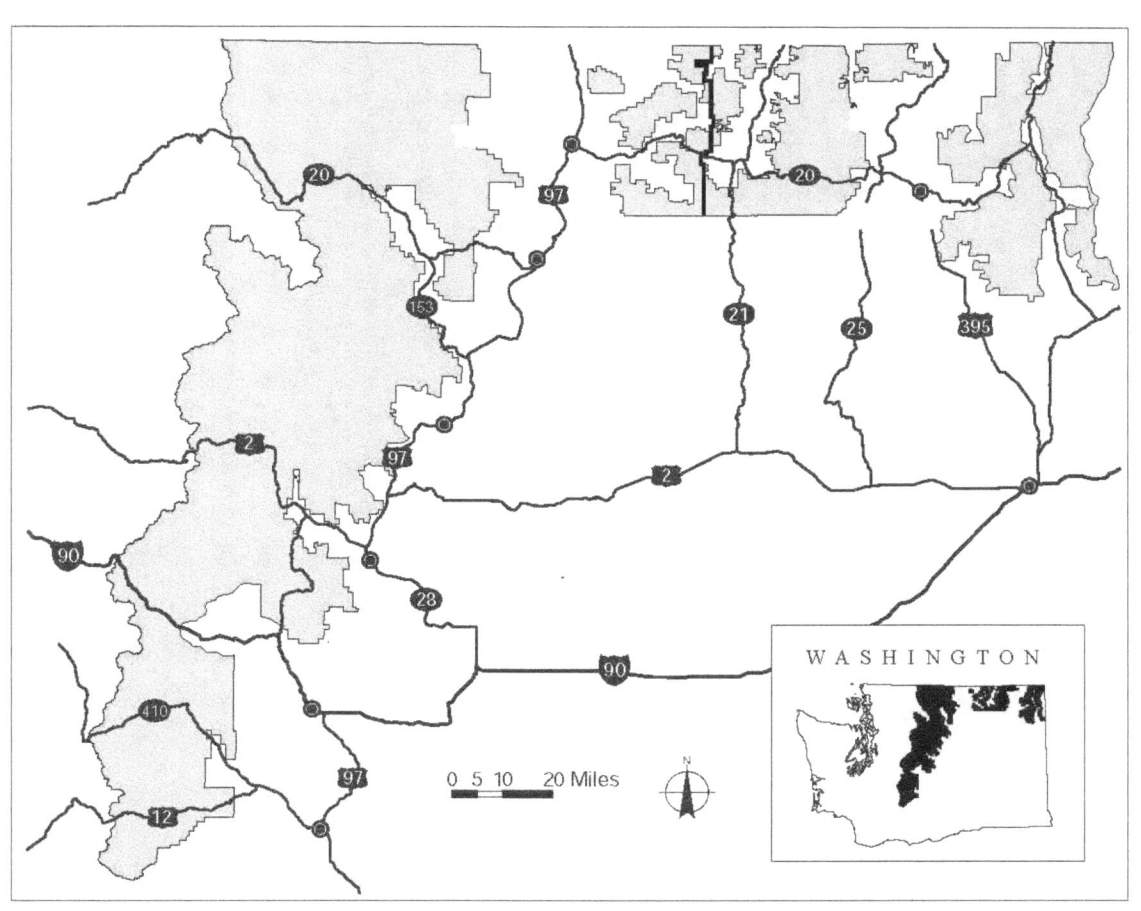

Authors

William L. Gaines is a wildlife ecologist, **Cameron A. Thomas** is an aquatic biologist, and **Richy J. Harrod** is a fire ecologist, Okanogan-Wenatchee National Forest, 215 Melody Lane, Wenatchee, WA 98801; **David W. Peterson** is a research forest ecologist, Forestry Sciences Laboratory, 1133 N Western Ave., Wenatchee, WA 98801.

Abstract

Gaines, William L.; Peterson, David W.; Thomas, Cameron A.; Harrod, Richy J. 2012. Adaptations to climate change: Colville and Okanogan-Wenatchee National Forests. Gen. Tech. Rep. PNW-GTR-862. Portland, OR: U.S. Department of Agriculture, Forest Service, Pacific Northwest Research Station. 34 p.

Forest managers are seeking practical guidance on how to adapt their current practices and, if necessary, their management goals, in response to climate change. Science-management collaboration was initiated on national forests in eastern Washington where resource managers showed a keen interest in science-based options for adapting to climate change at a 2-day workshop. Scientists and managers reviewed current climate change science and identified resources vulnerable to expected climate change. Vulnerabilities related to vegetation and habitat management included potential reductions in forest biodiversity and low forest resilience to changing disturbance regimes. The vulnerabilities related to aquatic and infrastructure resources included changing water quality and quantity, the risk to roads and other facilities from changes to hydrologic regimes, and the potential loss of at-risk aquatic species and habitats. Managers then worked in facilitated groups to identify adaptations that could be implemented through management and planning to reduce the vulnerability of key resources to climate change. The identified adaptations were grouped under two major headings: Increasing Ecological Resiliency to Climate Change, and Increasing Social and Economic Resiliency to Climate Change. The information generated from the science-management collaborative represents an initial and important step in identifying and prioritizing tangible steps to address climate change in forest management. Next would be the development of detailed implementation strategies that address the identified management adaptations.

Keywords: Science-management collaborative, Okanogan-Wenatchee National Forest, Colville National Forest, climate change, resource vulnerability, adaptations, resiliency.

Contents

Introduction

In 2008, Forest Service Chief Abigail R. Kimbell characterized the agency's response to the challenges presented by climate change as, "one of the most urgent tasks facing the Forest Service." Subsequently, Chief Tom Tidwell began an assertive program of action outlined in the agencywide "Strategic Framework for Responding to Climate Change" (USDA FS 2008a) that identified seven areas to address: (1) science development, (2) adaptation, (3) mitigation, (4) policy, (5) sustainable operations, (6) education, and (7) alliances with partners. Direction provided to forest and district planning teams further developed some of these emphasis areas. These include Forest Service Manual direction on ecological restoration and resilience (FSM 2000, Chapter 2020), and climate change considerations in project-level analysis (USDA FS 2008b).

In the 2010–2015 U.S. Department of Agriculture Strategic Plan, a strategic goal was established to "ensure our national forests and private working lands are conserved, restored, and made more resilient to climate change, while enhancing our water resources" (USDA 2010). Building upon this and the Strategic Framework, the Forest Service developed a "National Roadmap for Responding to Climate Change" and a "Climate Change Scorecard" (USDA FS 2010). The roadmap identified three types of actions that the Forest Service will take to respond to climate change: (1) assessing current risks, vulnerabilities, policies, and gaps in knowledge; (2) engaging internal and external partners in seeking solutions, such as science-management partnerships; and (3) managing for resilience, in ecosystems as well as in human communities, through adaptation, mitigation, and sustainable consumption strategies (USDA FS 2010). In this document, we address each of the actions identified in the roadmap through a science-management partnership to provide forest managers with an initial starting point to address climate change on two national forests.

Forest managers are seeking practical guidance on how to adapt their current practices and, if necessary, their management goals to address climate change concerns (Blate et al. 2009: Joyce et al. 2008; Ogden and Innes 2009; Peterson et al. 2011a, 2011b; Seppala et al. 2009; Spies et al. 2010). Adaptations to forest management would ideally reduce the negative impacts of climate changes and help managers take advantage of any positive impacts (Blate et al. 2009, Ogden and Innes 2009). However, it is currently a challenge for national forest and project-level planners to scale down both national-level policy and regional-scale climate science to address site-specific issues (Peterson et al. 2011). Provided in this report is information for the Okanogan-Wenatchee National Forest (OWNF) and Colville National Forest (CNF) that can be used in both national forest- and project-level planning.

Science-management collaboration was initiated on these two national forests in eastern Washington, where resource managers showed a keen interest in science-based options for adapting to climate change.

Science-management collaboration was initiated on these two national forests in eastern Washington, where resource managers showed a keen interest in science-based options for adapting to climate change following guidance in Peterson et al. (2011). Similar efforts have occurred on other national forests (Halosky et al. 2011) and guide forest management adaptations in Canada (Ogden and Innes 2009). Our work represents an initial effort of collaboration to develop specific concepts and applications that could potentially be implemented in management and planning to address climate change. This report (1) summarizes current climate change science relevant to eastern Washington, (2) describes the collaboration process, (3) describes for the OWNF and CNF the adaptation options for climate change identified from this effort, and (4) recommends development of further strategies that implement the highest priority adaptations (of those discussed).

Methods

Over a 2-day process, a focus group reviewed climate change information and elicited recommendations for adapting forest management. The first day focused on developing a scientific understanding of climate change and the potential effects to resources relevant to the OWNF and CNF. Scientists made presentations, and discussion occurred among scientists and resource management staff. The topics covered during the science presentations included:

Topic	Presentor(s)
Pacific Northwest climatic variability: past, present, and future	David L. Peterson, research ecologist, Pacific Northwest Research Station
Introduction to the concepts of vulnerability and adaptation	Jessica Halofsky, research ecologist, Pacific Northwest Research Station
Aquatics: snow and stream hydrology	Rick Woodsmith, aquatic ecologist, Pacific Northwest Research Station
Aquatics: aquatic biota	Karl Polivka, aquatic ecologist, Pacific Northwest Research Station
Vegetation	Dave W. Peterson, research forest ecologist, Pacific Northwest Research Station
Disturbances: insects and disease	Darci Carlson and Jim Hadfield, forest entomologist and pathologist, Okanogan-Wenatchee National Forest
Disturbances: fire	Dave W. Peterson, research forest ecologist, Pacific Northwest Research Station

Terrestrial wildlife	Bill Gaines, wildlife ecologist, Okanogan-Wenatchee National Forest, John Lehmkuhl, research wildlife biologist, Pacific Northwest Research Station
Landscape perspective	Paul Hessburg, landscape ecologist, Pacific Northwest Research Station

The second day focused on elicitation of feedback from OWNF and CNF resource managers about their concerns regarding climate change and recommendations for strategies and specific actions that would promote adaptation. The following questions were posed to resource managers:

Resource Vulnerability Questions

- How vulnerable is your resource area to anticipated future climate change?
- Where are the key areas of vulnerability (e.g., roads, invasive plants, lynx habitat, fire behavior in dry forests, loss of campgrounds, regeneration failures)?
- What aspect of future climate change creates the vulnerability (e.g., increased summer temperatures/drought, reduced winter snowpack, rain-on-snow events)?
- What is the level of vulnerability for each key area (e.g., high, medium, low)?
- What are the potential impacts of vulnerability (e.g., resource drain, failure of critical mission, loss of ecosystem service, threat to human health/safety, potential property losses)?

Adaptation and Mitigation Questions

- For each area of vulnerability, what management options exist for reducing vulnerability to future climate change (e.g., managing fuels to modify future wildfire behavior)?
- For each area of vulnerability, what management options exist for assisting the resource area to adjust to changing climate? Would these activities be implemented as part of normal work (proactive) or in response to some event or other trigger (reactive)?
- For the options described above, which of these are "no regrets" options that would be good resource management practices even if climate did not change as predicted?

The second day focused on elicitation of feedback from OWNF and CNF resource managers about their concerns regarding climate change and recommendations for strategies and specific actions that would promote adaptation.

- What information and tools are needed to address identified vulnerabilities? Are there any legal, policy, or management barriers to implementing proposed adaptation strategies?

Although the questions were addressed in the order listed, discussions were far ranging and often digressed to topics that had been discussed earlier. The scientists in attendance (the first three authors of this report) facilitated discussions and recorded responses from the group sessions. The responses were then summarized by topic and reviewed by OWNF and CNF staff for accuracy. In some cases, detail has been reduced in order to highlight the primary ideas and promote clarity.

Biogeographical Setting and Natural Resources

The Okanogan-Wenatchee and Colville National Forests (Forests) are located in north central and northeastern Washington state. The Forests are bounded on the west by the crest of the Cascade Range, on the north by the Canadian border, and on the east by the Idaho border. This area totals over 5 million acres of National Forest System lands spanning much of the eastern half of Washington state (fig. 1).

Colville National Forest

The 1.1-million-acre CNF in northeast Washington is bordered to the north by British Columbia, to the west by the Okanogan National Forest, to the east by the Idaho Panhandle National Forests, and to the south by a portion of the Colville Confederated Tribes Indian Reservation. The CNF has three ranger districts: Republic, Sullivan Lake-Newport, and Three Rivers. The forest headquarters is located in Colville.

Northeast Washington is geologically complex and includes the Columbia Basin and the Okanogan Highlands, which function as a transition zone between the Cascade and the Rocky Mountain Ranges. The major forest types that comprise the CNF include 11,900 acres of subalpine forest, 12,900 acres of cold-dry forest, 530,000 acres of cold-moist forest, 492,600 acres of dry forest, and 41,200 acres of mesic forest. About 16,850 acres of the CNF are other nonforest vegetation types. Most of the CNF was burned during the 1920s and 1930s, so the current forest is relatively young. Federally listed species include the endangered woodland caribou (*Rangifer tarandus*), threatened grizzly bear (*Ursus arctos*), and Canada lynx (*Lynx canadensis*). There are currently no federally listed plants on the Colville; however, the moonwort (*Botrychium lineare* W.H. Wagner) was determined to be warranted but precluded.

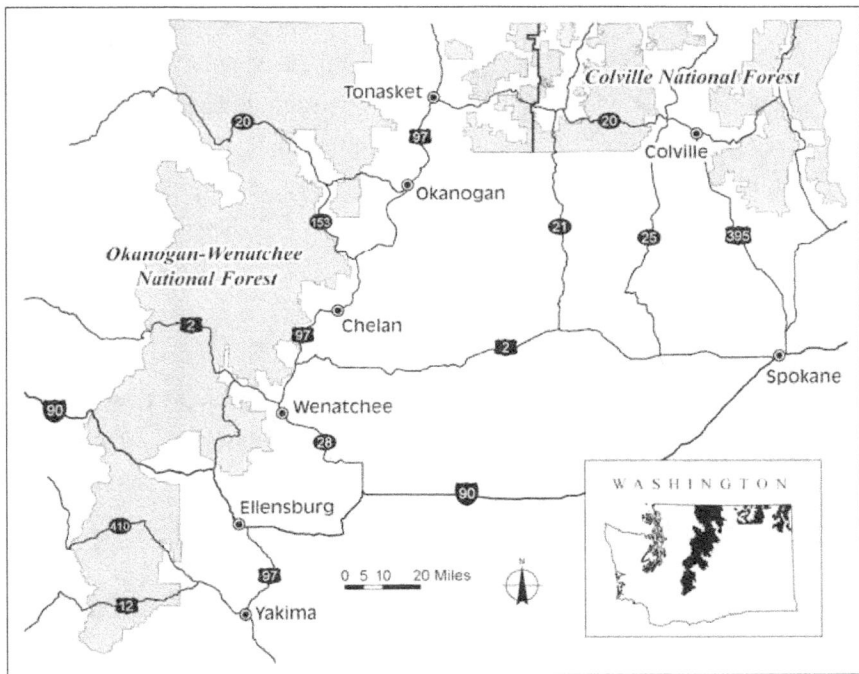

Figure 1—The climate change collaboration case study included the Colville National
Forest and the Okanogan-Wenatchee National Forest in eastern Washington.

Okanogan-Wenatchee National Forest

The OWNF encompasses 3.9 million acres of public land including about 1.4 million acres of designated wilderness. It includes seven ranger districts, with offices in Naches, Cle Elum, Leavenworth, Entiat, Chelan, Winthrop, and Tonasket. The Forest headquarters office is located in Wenatchee.

The major forest types that comprise the OWNF include 656,800 acres of subalpine forest, 329,700 acres of cold-dry forest, 1.5 million acres of cold-moist forest, 1.1 million acres of dry forest, and 214,700 acres of mesic forest. About 17,000 acres are identified as nonforested vegetation.

The Okanogan portion of the Forest is located in north central Washington state, and includes 1.7 million acres of public land, including portions of the Mount Baker-Snoqualmie National Forest. The Okanogan portion of the Forest is comprised of two distinct zones. The western zone includes the Methow Valley. Here, vegetation ranges from sagebrush (*Artemesia* spp.) lowlands, through the dry ponderosa pine (*Pinus ponderosa* C. Lawson), Douglas-fir (*Pseudotsuga mensiesii* (Mirb.) Franco), western larch (*Larix occidentalis* Nutt.), and cold-moist subalpine fir (*Abies lasiocarpa* (Hook.) Nutt.), Engleman spruce (*Picea engelmannii* Parry ex Engelm.) forests to timberline where whitebark pine (*Pinus albicaulis* Engelm.), and mountain hemlock (*Tsuga mertensiana* (Bong.) Carriere) share a scattered presence (Williams and Lillybridge 1983). The eastern zone, from the Meadows through the Okanogan Highlands, is drier with much less elevation gradient. Consequently, only the sagebrush and dry forest types are widely represented (Williams and Lillybridge 1983). Federally listed species include the endangered gray wolf (*Canis lupus*), threatened northern spotted owl (*Strix occidentalis caurina*), grizzly bear, and Canada lynx.

The Okanogan portion of the Forest includes land in Okanogan, Skagit, Whatcom, and Chelan Counties. Okanogan County covers most of the Forest. Forestry, grazing, and recreation are important to local economies and are supported by activities that occur on national forest lands. Water, an important resource provided by the national forest, supports the agricultural industry. Through special use permits, the Loup Loup Ski Bowl and an extensive network of cross-country ski trails provide winter recreation opportunities on national forest lands.

The Wenatchee portion of the Forest includes 2.2 million acres, stretching from Lake Chelan in the north to the Goat Rocks Wilderness in the south. It begins at the crest of the Cascade Range in central Washington and falls sharply to the breaks of the Columbia River. Elevations on the Wenatchee portion range from 800 to over 9,500 feet.

Geologic variety and great differences in amounts of precipitation throughout the Forest result in a diversity in vegetation and an associated richness of wildlife species. The vegetation changes with elevation and moisture as the Forest landscape rises from grassland and shrub-steppe vegetation in the low-lying eastern areas, through stands of ponderosa pine, and into mixed forests of pine, Douglas-fir, and larch (Lillybridge et al. 1995). At higher elevations and closer to the crest of the Cascade Range, subalpine areas support true firs and lodgepole pine, while alpine meadows support stands of alpine firs, larch, and whitebark pine (Lillybridge et al. 1995). Areas near the crest of the Cascade Range receive up to 140 inches of precipitation and as much as 25 feet of snow accumulation each year (Lillybridge et al. 1995). Moisture declines markedly from west to east, with less than 10 inches of precipitation falling annually on the eastern fringes of the Wenatchee portion of the OWNF. Federally listed wildlife species include the grizzly bear, northern spotted owl, Canada lynx, and gray wolf. There are two federally protected plants on the OWNF: the Wenatchee Mountains checker-mallow (*Sidalcea oregana* var. *calva*) and the showy stickseed (*Hackelia venusta* (Piper) H. St. John).

Policy, Planning, and Management Environments

Two overarching management plans set the standards and guidelines used to manage natural resources on the OWNF and CNF. The Northwest Forest Plan (NWFP) (USDA and USDI 1994) and amended existing land and resource management plans for national forests located within the range of the northern spotted owl. The NWFP includes all of the Wenatchee portion of the OWNF and the portion of the Okanogan that lies west and south of the Chewuch River. The remainder of the Okanogan portion of the OWNF and all of the Colville Forest are managed under the second management plan, the east-side screens (USDA FS 1998a). Both of these regional management plans recognized the need to protect and restore old-growth and late-successional forest habitat but used two different approaches. The NWFP accomplishes this through a system of reserves, which limit forest management activities to those that either maintain or promote the development of late-successional forest. There are 1.1 million acres (26 percent) of the OWNF within a system of 27 reserves (USDA FS 1997, 1998b). The east-side screens management plan promotes the development of old-growth and late-successional forests by managing toward the natural range of variation (Hessburg et al. 1997, 1999) and by limiting the cutting of trees to those less than 21 inches in diameter.

Observed and Anticipated Climatic Changes and Effects on Natural Resources

This section briefly summarizes observed and projected changes in atmospheric chemistry, the global climate system, and the climate of Washington state based on a review of current scientific literature. Also discussed are the influences these projected changes are likely to have on natural resources (e.g., water, vegetation, and wildlife) and disturbance regimes managed by national forests.

Regional Climate Change Overview

Atmospheric concentrations of carbon dioxide (CO_2) and other greenhouse gases have increased rapidly over the past century or more. Records from Mauna Loa Observatory in Hawaii (Keeling et al. 1995) show that global atmospheric concentrations of CO_2 rose by almost 17 percent during the period 1958 through 2005, from about 325 parts per million (ppm) to 380 ppm (IPCC 2007). Atmospheric CO_2 concentrations are expected to continue to rise for the foreseeable future, although future rates of increase may vary with changes in the global economy and the success or failure of international efforts to reduce or limit the growth of greenhouse gas emissions. Although atmospheric CO_2 concentrations are of concern primarily because of their potential to influence global temperatures (i.e., the "greenhouse

Temperatures have been increasing in Washington over the past century. In the last 100 years, temperatures have increased by about 1.5 °F.

effect"), higher CO_2 concentrations may also influence vegetation growth and water-use efficiency and are therefore linked more directly to forest ecosystem functioning and natural resource management.

Temperatures have been increasing in Washington over the past century. In the last 100 years, temperatures have increased by about 1.5 °F (Mote 2003b). The warming trends have been strongest in the winter months and weakest in the autumn months. Precipitation has also been increasing during the past century with the largest relative increases occurring during the spring in the eastern portion of the state (Mote 2003b).

The Climate Impacts Group at the University of Washington has projected future changes in climate of the Pacific Northwest based on climate projections produced for the Intergovernmental Panel on Climate Change (IPCC) fourth assessment report. They predict that temperatures will rise an average of 0.54 °F per decade over the next century (Elsner et al. 2009), a potentially much larger increase than experienced in the past 100 years. Predictions are for warming trends to be greater in the eastern part of the state. Precipitation projections for the region are more variable than temperature projections. In general, precipitation is predicted to increase in the winter and decrease in the summer (Mote et al. 2005a).

Winter temperatures play a large role in determining whether precipitation falls as snow or rain. Despite increases in precipitation in eastern Washington, warming temperatures have led to decreases in snowpack. Mote (2003a) reported reductions of 30 to 60 percent in April 1 snowpack from 1920 through 2000 over much of Washington (fig. 2). The largest decreases in snowpack have been at lower elevations (less than 5,900 feet). Projected temperature increases for the coming century are expected to increase the proportion of winter precipitation falling as rain, increase the frequency of winter flooding, reduce snowpack, increase winter streamflow, result in earlier peak flows, and decrease late spring and summer flows (Hamlet et al. 2007; Hamlet and Lettenmaier 1999; Mote et al. 2003a, 2003b, 2005a). The snowpack in the Cascades is projected to decrease by 44 percent by 2020 and by 58 percent by 2040 relative to the recent past. Peak runoff is expected to occur 4 to 6 weeks earlier (Climate Change Impacts Group 2004), while reduced summer streamflows will be more common and widespread (Climate Change Impacts Group 2004; Miles et al. 2000; Mote et al. 1999, 2003a, 2003b; Snover et al. 2003; Stewart et al. 2004). April 1 snow water equivalent is projected to decrease by an average of 27 to 29 percent across the state by the 2020s, 37 to 44 percent by the 2040s, and 53 to 65 percent by the 2080s (Elsner et al. 2009).

Figure 2—Percentage change in snowpack within the Pacific Northwest during 1920–2000 (http://cses.washington.edu/cig).

Disturbances

Since the mid 1980s, the size and intensity of large wildfires in the Western United States have increased markedly (Westerling et al. 2006). The frequency of large fires increased fourfold from 1970 through 1986 compared to 1987 through 2003. On average, the length of fire season has increased by 78 days over the same period. Westerling et al. (2006) attributed increases in large fires to reductions in fuel moisture driven by increased temperatures and lower snowpack. In addition, the increase in fire severity and risk has been driven in part by increased fuel loads because of fire suppression practices (McKenzie et al. 2004).

The predicted increases in spring and summer temperature will exacerbate the frequency and intensity of disturbances such as fire (McKenzie et al. 2004, Wotton and Flannigan 1993) (Littell et al. 2009). Some forest insects have already expanded their ranges northward, and others have switched from a 2-year to a 1-year life cycle, increasing the probability of large outbreaks (Logan and Powell 2001, Logan

Since the mid 1980s, the size and intensity of large wildfires in the Western United States have increased markedly. The predicted increases in spring and summer temperature will exacerbate the frequency and intensity of disturbances such as fire and forest insects.

et al. 2003). Mountain pine beetle (*Dendroctonus ponderosae*) populations are expected to become more viable at higher elevations, leading to increased incidence of mountain pine beetle outbreaks (Littell et al. 2009).

Even under relatively modest greenhouse gas emissions scenarios, there may be a doubling in the area burned in Western States (McKenzie et al. 2004). In the interior Columbia Basin, Littell et al. (2009) predicted that the area burned is likely to double or even triple by the end of the 2040s. Models predict an increase in the length of the fire season and in the likelihood of fires east of the Cascade Range (Bachelet et al. 2001, McKenzie et al. 2004). The higher rates of disturbance by fires and insects are likely to be more significant agents of change in forest structure and composition in the 21st century than species turnover or declines in productivity (Littell et al. 2009). This suggests that understanding future disturbance regimes is critical for successful adaptation to climate change.

Hydrology and Fish

Vano et al. (2009) modeled the effects of climate change on water availability within the Yakima River basin. They found that water shortages occurred historically in 14 percent of the years. The percentage of years with water shortages was projected to increase to 27 to 32 percent in the 2020s, 33 to 36 percent in the 2040s, and 50 to 77 percent in the 2080s. These projections for reduced water availability are a result of predictions for earlier and reduced spring snowmelt as the century progresses (Vano et al. 2009).

Climate change is expected to increasingly alter stream function on the OWNF and CNF based on studies that have considered the effects of climate change for the Columbia River basin. A review of scientific information completed by the Independent Scientific Advisory Board (ISAB)(ISAB 2007) identified numerous consequences. Bisson (2008) summarized expected changes in the ISAB report as follows: (1) warmer temperatures will result in more precipitation falling as rain rather than snow; (2) snowpack will diminish and streamflow timing will be altered; (3) peak river flows will likely increase; and (4) water temperatures will continue to rise (fig. 3).

In addition to an increase in large flood events, wildfires and forest insect outbreaks are also expected to increase as noted earlier. Fish habitat in some instances will respond favorably to these events as they are likely to reconnect flood plains and increase large wood accumulations, which, in combination, will increase stream channel complexity (Bisson 2008). Depending on landscape position, stream habitat and dependent species such as trout and salmon might also experience negative consequences resulting from climate change. A higher frequency of severe

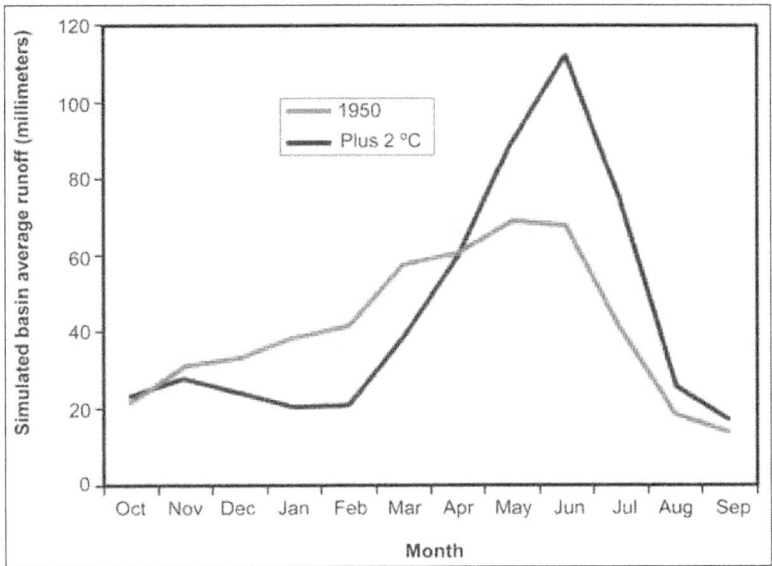

Figure 3—Reduced snowpack and earlier runoff alter peak and base flows in the Naches River basin (http://cses.washington.edu/cig). The blue line represents historical flow regime in 1950, and the red line is a modeled flow regime based on a 2 °C increase in temperature.

floods will scour streambeds and reduce spawning success for fall spawning fish (Bisson 2008). Decreasing snowpacks and earlier spring runoff will affect migration patterns for salmon that could further affect their survival in the ocean (Mote et al. 2003a, Pearcy 1997). Summer base flows are expected to be lower and last longer, which would shrink available habitat, forcing fish into smaller and less diverse habitat (Battin et al. 2007, Bisson 2008). Additionally, summer temperatures in some stream locations that currently support salmon and trout could rise to a point where they become lethal (Crozier et al. 2008). Higher stream temperatures will likely favor nonsalmonid species that are better adapted to warmer water, including potential predators and competitors (Reeves et al. 1987, Sanderson et al. 2009).

Mantua et al. (2009) evaluated the sensitivity of freshwater habitat of Pacific salmon (*Oncorhynchus* spp.) to climate change. They found that predicted increases in stream temperatures will only slightly increase thermal stress for salmon in eastern Washington for the 2020s, but thermal stress will increase as the century progresses. Streamflow simulations predict that the largest hydrologic sensitivities are for watersheds that currently have a mix of direct runoff from autumn rainfall and springtime snowmelt (transient watersheds). The combined effects of warming stream temperatures and altered streamflows will very likely reduce reproductive success for many salmon populations, but impacts will differ according to different

Habitat restoration and protection can help to mitigate some of the anticipated effects of climate change; however, habitat deterioration associated with climate change will make salmon recovery targets more difficult to attain.

life-history types and watershed types. Salmon populations having a stream-type life history with extended freshwater rearing periods (steelhead, *Oncorhynchus mykiss*; coho, *O. kisutch*; sockeye, *O. nerka*; stream-type Chinook, *O. tshawytscha*; bull trout, *Salvelinus confluentus*) are predicted to experience large increases in hydrologic and thermal stress in summer owing to diminishing streamflow and increasing water temperatures. Salmon with an ocean-type life history are predicted to experience the greatest freshwater productivity declines in transient runoff watersheds where future warming is predicted to increase the magnitude and frequency of winter flooding that will reduce egg-to-fry survival rates (Mantua et al. 2009). Habitat restoration and protection can help to mitigate some of the anticipated effects of climate change; however, habitat deterioration associated with climate change will make salmon recovery targets more difficult to attain (Battin et al. 2007).

Vegetation

Climate change is expected to alter the distribution of forests, with a trend that is generally upward in elevation and northerly in latitude. Climate change will likely have the greatest effect at forest boundaries, both at the upper and lower elevations of forest distribution. At high elevations, seedling establishment and tree growth may be enhanced by warmer temperatures and decreased snowpack (Bachelet et al. 2001; Franklin et al. 1971; Nakawatase and Peterson 2006; Peterson and Peterson 1994, 2001; Peterson et al. 2002; Woodward et al. 1995). Thus, expansions of forests into the alpine zones should be expected. Conversely, at lower elevations, decreased summer precipitation, decreased snowpack, and increased temperatures have the potential to shift treeline up in elevation (Mote et al. 2003b, Neilson et al. 2005).

However, these simple predictions of forest response to climate change do not account for other factors that may influence forests. For example, the upslope contraction of eastern Washington forests in response to warmer and drier conditions may be offset by increased water-use efficiency resulting from increased atmospheric CO_2 concentrations (Bachelet et al. 2001, Krajick 2004). Models that consider this CO_2 effect predict expansions of forests into lower elevations (Daly et al. 2000, Neilson and Drapek 1998).

Littell et al. (2009) studied the potential impacts of climate change on forests of Washington. They predicted that by the mid-21st century, some areas of the interior Columbia Basin and eastern Cascade Range are likely to experience substantial declines in climatically suitable areas for Douglas-fir, particularly in the Okanogan Highlands. In addition, they projected increased climate-related stress to pine tree species, and increased susceptibility to mountain pine beetle.

In eastern Washington, there is a strong interaction between climate-induced changes in disturbances and changes to vegetation in fire-prone ecosystems. Climate-driven changes in fire regimes will likely be the dominant driver of change in Western U.S. forests over the next century (McKenzie et al. 2004). This is especially true in eastern Washington forests where increased temperatures, reduced snowpack and summer precipitation, and increased fuel loads from fire exclusion create conditions for increased large fire occurrences.

Wildlife

The anticipated climatic changes to eastern Washington environments described in the preceding sections are likely to result in a variety of effects to wildlife populations and their habitats. A striking conclusion reached from reviewed climate change literature was the degree of change to wildlife habitats and populations that has already occurred and been documented (Lawler and Mathias 2007, Root et al. 2003). The remainder of this section is devoted to describing the effects that changing climates are likely to have, or already have had on wildlife populations and habitats. While not all of the studies used to exemplify these effects occurred in eastern Washington, they do address species relevant to eastern Washington and provide insights into the kinds of changes for which planning is needed.

Changes in species distributions—
As environments adjust to changing climate, species will shift their distributions in order to find suitable conditions to carry out various life history stages. Some birds have been shifting their ranges both poleward in latitude and upward in elevation in response to warming climates (Root 1992, 1993; Thomas and Lennon 1999). The most extensive predictions about how species distributions are likely to change because of climate change have been made for land birds (Price 2002, Wormworth and Mallon 2006). Table 1 shows predicted changes in species distributions (based on Price 2002) for bird species common to the dry and mesic forests of eastern Washington. The list of species was developed from monitoring studies conducted in the dry and mesic forests of eastern Washington (Gaines et al. 2007, 2009, 2010).

Gonzalez et al. (2007) provide an example of predicted changes in the habitat distribution for the Canada lynx (*Lynx canadensis*). They modeled lynx habitat based on the distribution of boreal forest and snow cover, and predicted that suitable conditions for lynx habitat may shift as far as 120 miles northward. Their analysis suggested that these changes in lynx habitat would affect peninsular populations and predicted that habitat in the Okanogan and Wenatchee mountains, and presumably the Kettle Crest, would be vulnerable to climate change in the long term.

Climate-driven changes in fire regimes will likely be the dominant driver of change in Western U.S. forests over the next century. This is especially true in eastern Washington forests where increased temperatures, reduced snowpack and summer precipitation, and increased fuel loads from fire exclusion create conditions for increased large fire occurrences.

Table 1—Predicted changes in the distribution of some bird species associated with dry and mesic forests, eastern Washington[a]

May exclude	May contract	Little change
Mountain chickadee (*Parus gambeli*)	Chipping sparrow (*Spizella passerina*)	Brown-headed cowbird (*Molothrus ater*)
Townsend's warbler (*Dendroica townsendi*)	Dark-eyed junco (*Junco hyemalis*)	Spotted towhee (*Pipilo erythrophthalmus*)
Hammond's flycatcher (*Empidonax hammondii*)	Nashville warbler (*Vermivora ruficapilla*)	Purple finch (*Carpodacus purpureus*)
Cassin's finch (*Carpodacus cassinni*)	MacGillivray's warbler (*Oporornis tolmiei*)	Western tanager (*Piranga ludoviciana*)
Red crossbill (*Loxia curvirostra*)	Yellow-rumped warbler (*Dendroica magnolia*)	
	Cassin's vireo (*Vireo cassinii*)	
	Red-breasted nuthatch (*Sitta canadensis*)	
	Dusky flycatcher (*Empidonax oberholseri*)	
	Pine siskin (*Carduelis pinus*)	
	Warbling vireo (*Vireo olivaceus*)	

[a] The species list is based on surveys described in Gaines et al. 2009a. The predicted changes in distribution are based on Price 2002.

Changes in the timing of breeding and other activities—
Blaustein et al. (2001) studied the onset of breeding by western toads (*Bufo boreas*) and Cascades frogs (*Rana cascadae*). They showed that earlier breeding was related to warmer water temperatures and lower mountain snowpack (fig. 4). Breeding of tree swallows (*Tachycineta bicolor*) has been documented to begin 5 to 9 days earlier across North America, related to increasing average May temperatures (Dunn and Winkler 1999).

Changes in pathogens and invasive species distributions—
Outbreaks of the pathogen *Saprolegnia ferax* have been documented in western toads and Cascades frogs (Kiesecker et al. 2001). These outbreaks are due to increased UV-B exposure and have been identified as a cause of high mortality in amphibian embryos in the Pacific Northwest. Amphibians, particularly those that breed in shallow montane lakes and ponds, may be quite susceptible to climate-induced changes in UV-B exposure (Kiesecker et al. 2001).

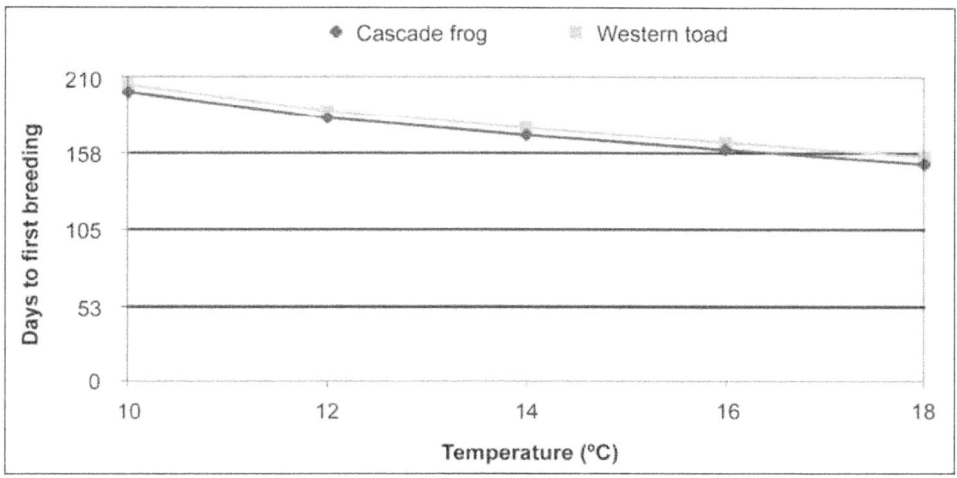

Figure 4—The earlier onset of breeding in Cascade frog and western toad populations as temperature increases (based on Blaunstein et al. 2001).

Changes in survival and extinction risks—

Some species will be better able to adjust to climate-induced changes to their habitats than will others. In general, species with limited distributions, limited dispersal abilities, highly specialized habitat needs, and with already at-risk populations are likely to be the most vulnerable (Thomas et al. 2004). One of the best documented examples of increased risk of extinction because of climate change is the American pika (*Ochotona princeps*). Pika populations throughout the inland West have already experienced several extinctions over the last 50 years (Beever et al. 2003, Root et al. 2003). Pikas have characteristics that make them vulnerable to climate change: they do not move large distances (less than 0.62 mile); their habitat generally occurs in small, isolated patches; they do not use burrows that could dampen extreme temperatures, and are densely furred so they do not dissipate heat easily. Other species that occur on the OWNF or CNF that may be vulnerable to extirpation owing to their limited distributions include the Chelan mountainsnail (*Oreohelix* sp. and other *Oreohelix* spp.) (Burke 1999, Gaines et al. 2005, Weaver et al. 2009) and woodland caribou (Apps and McLellan 2006).

Changes in interactions among species—

Community-level effects and interactions are difficult to study and predict because they have to account for individual responses of many species simultaneously. Resulting from differential species responses, terrestrial communities are likely to be restructured (Graham and Grimm 1990), altering interspecific interactions, such as competition, predation, nest parasitism, etc. For example, the complex relationships that occur among species within late-successional forests in eastern

Washington are just beginning to be understood. Northern spotted owls compete with barred owls (*Strix varia*) for space and resources (Singleton et al. 2010). The primary prey species of the spotted owl includes the northern flying squirrel (*Glaucomys sabrinus*) whose populations depend on the abundance of lichens and truffles (Lehmkuhl 2004; Lehmkuhl et al. 2004, 2006). It is unknown how climate change will affect this chain of interactions, but it is likely that different species within the community will react differently, altering the community structure and our understanding of how the community functions.

To really understand how communities of species are likely to be restructured by climate change, models must include more than just changes in the distribution of habitats. Niche modeling that includes multiple species and multiple interactions (such as climate and vegetation) (Carroll 2010) will be needed, and this is challenging when little is known about many species (Kickert et al. 1999).

Resource Vulnerabilities

Based on the scientific understanding developed on the first day of the 2-day climate change workshop, participants were asked to identify and rank resources (as high, moderate, or low) in relation to perceived vulnerability to climate change (table 2). Vulnerability was defined as the extent to which a natural or social system is susceptible to sustained damage from weather extremes, climate variability, and change (and other interactive stressors) (table 3, Binder et al. 2009). Vulnerabilities were categorized into those related to the management of vegetation and habitats, and those related to aquatics and infrastructure. The vulnerabilities related to vegetation and habitat management included two general themes: the conservation of biodiversity, and the restoration of resilient forests and disturbance regimes. The vulnerabilities related to aquatic and infrastructure resources included water quality and quantity, the risk to roads and other facilities from changes to hydrologic regimes, and at-risk aquatic species and habitats. The next section addresses potential adaptations that address these vulnerabilities.

Adapting to Climate Change Through Management and Planning

Forest managers present at the workshop identified vulnerabilities and adaptive strategies that could be implemented to address the vulnerabilities. The goal of these strategies is to make human and natural systems more resilient to the impacts of climate change (Binder et al. 2009, Millar et al. 2007). A resilient system is one that has the capacity to absorb and rebound from weather extremes, climate variability, or change while continuing to function (Binder et al. 2009, IPCC

Forest managers present at the workshop identified vulnerabilities and adaptive strategies that could be implemented to address the vulnerabilities.

Table 2—Low, moderate, and high vulnerabilities identified by forest managers at the 2008 climate change workshop, Colville and Okanogan-Wenatchee National Forests

Resource vulnerability area	Ranking	Vulnerability
Vegetation and habitat	High	• Plant migration could reduce the availability of whitebark pine and shift the location of other forest types reducing the availability of alpine habitats.
		• Habitat specialists (caribou, lynx, and wolverine (*Gulo gulo*) denning habitat) will have the most difficult time adjusting.
		• Riparian and wetland habitats may be particularly vulnerable.
		• Habitat connectivity will be reduced for some species and may be most detrimental for low-mobility habitat specialists.
		• Dry forest stands with high tree densities and fuel loads become increasingly susceptible to fire, insects, disease, and drought.
		• Larger and more frequent disturbances could make it difficult for forests/habitats to recover and cause them to be more susceptible to invasive species.
		• Past management for timber production and fire exclusion has made old forests more susceptible to fire, including severe fire.
		• Species with narrow ecological amplitude and endemics may be at high risk for local extinction.
	Moderate	• Elk and deer may be vulnerable to increased diseases.
		• Species on the edges of their ranges or with limited mobility may be at risk for local extinction. We need to assess whether or not these are "lost causes" before investing in their conservation.
	Low	• Habitat generalists (grizzly bear, wolves, red squirrel, black bear) that are more mobile may fair better.
		• Increased carbon dioxide might increase growth of already overstocked stands.
Aquatic and infrastructure	High	• Municipal/agricultural watersheds may lose the capacity to deliver water at current levels.
		• Reduced cold water in streams could reduce fish habitat availability and alter the timing of spawning or the ability of fish to spawn.
		• Roads and other facilities could be threatened by increased frequency of extreme hydrologic events such as floods and debris flows.
		• Some aquatic species could become more susceptible to disease and changes in stream productivity.
		• Water availability for ecosystem processes (e.g., soil water for plant growth) could be reduced or shifted seasonally.

Table 2—Low, moderate, and high vulnerabilities identified by forest managers at the 2008 climate change workshop, Colville and Okanogan-Wenatchee National Forests (continued)

Resource vulnerability area	Ranking	Vulnerability
Aquatic and infrastructure	Moderate	• Ski area operation could be affected by reduced winter snowpack.
		• Riparian areas could become harder to manage as stream networks become smaller and less connected (loss of perennial headwater streams).
		• Grazing allotments may be changed owing to changes in water availability and forage productivity.
		• Cultural sites may be sensitive to increased fire.
	Low	• Sustaining tribal use areas may become more difficult as resources become scarcer.
		• Roads may require more maintenance owing to increased use. Facilities may receive greater use (and wear) from longer recreational seasons.

Source: Binder et al. 2009.

Table 3—Basic concepts in adaptation planning

Stressors	Definition
Sensitivity	The degree to which a system is affected, either negatively or positively, by climate variability or change. The effect may be direct or indirect.
Exposure	The nature and degree to which a system is exposed to significant climatic variations. Exposure to climatic stresses may vary by geography, elevation, length of time, and other factors.
Vulnerability	The extent to which a natural or social system is susceptible to sustained damage from weather extremes, climate variability, and change (and other interactive stressors).
Adaptive capacity	The ability of a system to adjust to climate stresses (including weather extremes, climate variability, and climate change) so that potential damages are reduced, consequences coped with, or opportunities maximized.
Restoration	Putting or bringing back into a former, normal, unimpaired state or condition.
Resilience	The ability of an ecosystem to respond to disturbance. The concept is commonly used and incorporates the idea of resistance to disturbance as well as the time it takes a system to respond.

Source: Binder et al. 2009.

2007, Turner et al. 2003). The concept of a resilient system has been applied to both ecological and social systems (O'Brien et al. 2009, Folke 2006). The identified adaptations were grouped under two major headings: Increasing Ecological Resiliency to Climate Change, and Increasing Social and Economic Resiliency to Climate Change.

Increasing Ecological Resiliency to Climate Change

Generally, conservation efforts of the recent past have taken a static approach to conserving biodiversity and protecting ecological systems (Millar 2008). Usually this has involved the delineation of a system of reserves (Heller and Zavaleta 2009, Spies et al. 2006), or the restoration of the landscape to a historical condition (Landres et al. 1999). Areas selected to protect ecosystems today may not protect ecosystems in a future altered by climate change (Bengtsson et al. 2003, Carroll et al. 2009, Hannah and Salm 2004, Heller and Zavaleta 2009, Pearsons et al. 1992). Increasing ecological resiliency will require landscape planning to determine restoration priorities, restoration of ecosystems in anticipation of future disturbance regimes, better tools to predict climate change effects, and the ability to monitor and adapt strategies relatively quickly as conditions change (Heller and Zavaleta 2009). Following are the strategies identified by the work groups to increase ecological resiliency:

Restore landscape resiliency—

- Use landscape-level planning to identify restoration treatment areas, the most effective locations to reduce fire flow, to restore patch sizes, and to sustain wildlife habitats (Agar et al. 2007, Finney 2004, Franklin et al. 2008, Perry et al. 2011, Peterson et al. 2011b, Spies et al. 2010).
- Use landscape-level planning to evaluate the interaction between hydrologic regimes and infrastructure such as roads. Identify significant problem areas (areas where access is needed for treatments, recreation, etc.) and prioritize road restoration opportunities (Ogden and Innes 2009, Peterson et al. 2011b).
- Conduct landscape planning across ownerships in order to evaluate patterns, processes, and functions (Franklin et al. 2008; Heller and Zavaleta 2009, Hessburg et al. 2005, 2007).
- Use the range of variation (historical and future) to determine where treatments are needed and to restore landscape pattern, functions, and processes (see Hessburg et al. 2005 for a description of the historical range of variation, and Gartner et al. 2008 for a description of the future range of variation).

Increasing ecological resiliency will require landscape planning to determine restoration priorities, restoration of ecosystems in anticipation of future disturbance regimes, better tools to predict climate change effects, and the ability to monitor and adapt strategies relatively quickly as conditions change.

- Match treatment unit sizes with desired patch sizes determined from landscape level planning (Hessburg et al. 2005, 2007; Perry et al. 2011).

Restore forest patch resiliency—

- Use the range of variation (historical and future) to guide patch-level restoration of species composition, structure, and spatial pattern (Franklin et al. 2008, Harrod et al. 1999, Spies et al. 2010).
- Use thinning (mechanical and through prescribed fire) to reduce biomass, provide more vigorous growing conditions, and reduce vulnerability to uncharacteristic wildfire and epidemic insect outbreaks (Franklin et al. 2008, Hessburg et al. 2005, Spies et al. 2010).
- Retain the most fire-tolerant tree species and size classes commensurate with the forest type (Franklin et al. 2008, Harrod et al. 1999, Perry et al. 2011).
- Retain and restore old- and large-tree structures because they are the most difficult to replace and most resilient to disturbances (Franklin et al. 2008, Harrod et al. 1999, Hessburg et al. 2005).
- Minimize soil disturbance and restore soil productivity (Ogden and Innes 2009).

Maintain or restore biological diversity—

- Implement the restoration strategy for whitebark pine (Aubry et al. 2008).
- Provide for habitat connectivity (fish, plants, and wildlife) so that species can adjust their ranges to changes brought about by changing climates (Heller and Zavaleta 2009, Opdam and Wascher 2004, Parmesan 2006, Spies et al. 2010).
- Restore beaver (*Castor canadensis*) populations to increase water storage and retain wetlands (Brown 2008).
- Protect cold-water areas, as they are important refugia for at-risk fish species (Mantua et al. 2009, Spies et al. 2010).
- Reduce the impacts of roads on wetland and riparian habitats (Battin et al. 2007, Ogden and Innes 2009).

Implement early detection rapid response for invasive species—

- Implement integrated pest management to treat existing and new populations (Peterson et al. 2011b).
- Focus on treating small problems before they become large, unsolvable problems. Recognize that proactive management is more effective than delayed implementation (Halofsky et al. 2011, Peterson et al. 2011b).

Treat landscape disturbances as management opportunities—

- Plan for postdisturbance recovery. Because large fires and other disturbances are expected periodic occurrences, incorporating them into the planning process will encourage postdisturbance management actions that take climate into account, rather than treating disturbance as an anomaly or crisis (Halofsky et al. 2011, Peterson et al. 2011b, Spies et al. 2010).
- Develop more dynamic approaches to recovery after a major disturbance as standard postfire management practices are typically not climate-proactive (Peterson et al. 2011b).

Increasing Social and Economic Resiliency to Climate Change

The following strategies are intended to reduce impacts of climate change on forest infrastructure that would cause and, in some cases, already has caused, expensive repairs, temporary closures, etc. These impacts are anticipated on account of changes in the hydrologic regimes brought about by climate change. In addition, these strategies are intended to educate forest employees and the public about climate change and provide support for collaborative learning that facilitates adaptive management.

Match infrastructure to expected future conditions—

- Reduce the impacts of roads on water quality, quantity, and flow regimes (Binder et al. 2009, Ogden and Innes 2009, Peterson et al. 2011b).
- Decouple roads, or remove roads that interrupt hydrologic function (Binder et al. 2009).
- Relocate roads and other structures that are at risk from increased peak flows (Ogden and Innes 2009, Woodsmith 2008).

Promote education and awareness about climate change—

- Educate employees about climate change science and adaptations (Binder et al. 2009; Heller and Zavaleta 2009; Peterson et al. 2011a, 2011b).
- Proactively engage the public in an education program that increases understanding of the need for adaptation (Binder et al. 2009; Peterson et al. 2011a, 2011b).
- Develop educational materials and programs about climate change.

Collaborate to implement adaptive management strategies—

- Monitoring and adaptive management will be critical to understanding how strategies are working and if adaptations are needed (Binder et al. 2009; Heller and Zavaleta 2009; Millar et al. 2007; Peterson et al. 2011a, 2011b; Spies et al. 2010).

These strategies are intended to educate forest employees and the public about climate change and provide support for collaborative learning that facilitates adaptive management.

- A high level of collaboration between research and management will be necessary to integrate evolving science understanding and to design and implement monitoring (Heller and Zavaleta 2009, Peterson et al. 2011a).
- Planning across jurisdictional boundaries and collaboration on projects across boundaries will be vital to successfully adapting to climate change and creating more resilient forest and human systems (Heller and Zavaleta 2009, Peterson et al. 2011b).

Information and Tool Needs

The primary information and tools that managers identified during the workshop included models to better predict climate change impacts to resources and to evaluate management options. There was considerable discussion concerning how to develop a scientifically credible monitoring program with a concise and realistic set of variables that are important in monitoring climate change.

Managers identified the following tools that would be useful to better predict climate change impacts and understand the effectiveness of management options:

- Tools and expertise to evaluate fire flow over landscapes, and to identify strategic locations on the landscape where treatments are most effective at reducing unwanted fire effects.
- Tools and an approach to evaluate landscapes to determine past, current, and future vegetation patterns (cover types, structure stages), processes (fire, insects), and functions (wildlife habitats).
- Models to predict the movement of plant and animal species, and the potential effects of climate change on species distribution (Heller and Zavaleta 2009).
- Models to predict the timing and intensity of peak flows and to determine channel maintenance flows.
- Location of areas that will likely provide refugia for fish.

Managers identified a need to develop a comprehensive monitoring plan to deal with climate change. Monitoring would be a collaborative effort between science, management, and stakeholders. Some specific items for monitoring that were identified included:

- Monitor the effectiveness of weed treatments.
- Monitor whitebark pine as it is highly vulnerable to climate change.
- Monitor fish populations and habitat across broad areas.
- Monitor wildlife populations to determine the effectiveness of conservation strategies and recovery plans.
- Identify and monitor key indicators of climate change.

Managers identified a need to develop a comprehensive monitoring plan to deal with climate change. Monitoring would be a collaborative effort between science, management, and stakeholders.

Conclusions

We summarized the best available science relevant to climate change and the potential effects of climate change on eastern Washington forest environments. With this knowledge base, forest managers identified resource vulnerabilities and potential adaptations to management that can address anticipated climate change impacts. We identified four primary areas of adaptation strategies: (1) increase patch- and landscape-level forest resiliency through aggressive restoration based on understanding of the natural range of variation and projected effects of changing climate on the range of variation; (2) restore hydrologic function and fish passage in priority areas where water interacts with roads and other infrastructure; (3) increase employee and public awareness of the potential impacts of climate change on forest resources and the adaptations being implemented to address them; and (4) owing to the high degree of uncertainty associated with climate change predictions and the effectiveness of adaptations, develop an adaptive management approach that relies of rigorous monitoring and research.

A workshop participant provided a quote that thoughtfully and succinctly defines what lies ahead: "To deal with climate change will require a new level of focus, meaning some things will have to fall off the plate. The scale and immediacy of climate change is different from past challenges."

"To deal with climate change will require a new level of focus, meaning some things will have to fall off the plate. The scale and immediacy of climate change is different from past challenges."

Acknowledgments

We are extremely grateful to the employees of the Okanogan-Wenatchee and Colville National Forests who participated in this workshop. We are equally grateful to the scientists from the Pacific Northwest Research Station who so willingly shared their expertise at the 2008 workshop. D.L. Peterson and K. O'Halloran provided valuable advice on the organization of the workshop. D.L. Peterson, K. O'Halloran, and J. Hadfield provided thorough and thoughtful reviews of this manuscript. B. Fish and C. Wilson made numerous editorial suggestions that greatly enhanced this report. Funding for the development of this manuscript was generously provided by the Pacific Northwest Region Climate Change Coordinator.

Metric Equivalents

When you know:	Multiply by:	To get:
Inches	2.54	Centimeters
Feet	0.305	Meters
Miles	1.609	Kilometers
Acres	0.405	Hectares
Degrees Fahrenheit	0.55(°F-32)	Degree celsius

Literature Cited

Agar, A.A.; Finney, M.A.; Kerns, B.K.; Maffei, H. 2007. Modeling wildfire risk to northern spotted owl *(Strix occidentalis caurina)* in central Oregon, USA. Forest Ecology and Management. 246: 45–56.

Apps, C.D.; McLellan, B.N. 2006. Factors influencing the dispersion and fragmentation of endangered mountain caribou populations. Biological Conservation. 130: 84–97.

Aubry, C.; Goheen, D.; Shoal, R.; Ohlson, T.; Lorenz, T.; Bower, A.; Mehmel, C.; Sniezko, R. 2008. Whitebark pine restoration strategy for the Pacific Northwest Region. Portland, OR: U.S. Department of Agriculture, Forest Service, Pacific Northwest Region. 90 p. + appendixes.

Bachelet, D.; Neilson, R.P.; Lenihan, J.M.; Drapek, R.J. 2001. Climate change effects on vegetation distribution and carbon budget in the United States. Ecosystems. 4: 164–185.

Battin, J.; Wiley, M.W.; Ruckelshaus, M.H.; Palmer, R.N.; Korb, E.; Bartz, K.K. 2007. Projected impacts of climate change on salmon habitat restoration. Proceedings of the National Academy of Sciences. 104(16): 6720–6725.

Beever, E.A.; Brussard, P.F.; Berger, J. 2003. Patterns of apparent extirpation among isolated populations of pikas *(Ochotona princeps)* in the Great Basin. Journal of Mammalogy. 84: 37–54.

Bengtsson, J.; Angelstam, P.; Elmqvist, T. 2003. Reserves, resilience and dynamic landscapes. Ambio. 32: 389–396.

Binder, L.C.W.; Barcelos, J.K.; Booth, D.B. [et al.]. 2009. Preparing for climate change in Washington state. In: Elsner, M.M.; Littel, J.; Binder, L.W., eds. The Washington Climate Change Impacts Assessment. Seattle, WA: Center for Science in the Earth System, University of Washington: 373–407.

Bisson, P. 2008. Salmon and trout in the Pacific Northwest and climate change. http://www.fs.fed.us/ccrc/topics/salmon-trout.shtml. (June 16, 2008).

Blate, G.M.; Joyce, L.A.; Littell, J.S.; McNulty, S.G.; Millar, C.I.; Moser, S.C.; Neilson, R.P.; O'Halloran, K.; Peterson, D.L. 2009. Adapting to climate change in United States national forests. Unasylva. 231/232(60): 57–62.

Blaustein, A.R.; Belden, L.K.; Olson, D.H.; Green, D.M.; Root, T.L.; Kiesecker, J.M. 2001. Amphibian breeding and climate change. Conservation Biology. 15(6): 1804–1809.

Brown, R. 2008. Implications of climate change for conservation, restoration, and management of national forest lands. Washington, DC: Defenders of Wildlife. 32 p.

Burke, T.; Applegarth, J.S.; Weasma, T.R. 1999. Management recommendations for Survey and Manage terrestrial mollusks. Portland, OR: U.S. Department of Agriculture, Forest Service, Pacific Northwest Region. 22 p.

Carroll, C.; Dunk, J.R.; Moilanen, A. 2009. Optimizing resiliency of reserve networks to climate change: multispecies conservation planning in the Pacific Northwest, USA. Global Change Biology.

Carroll, C. 2010. Role of climatic niche models in focal-species-based conservation planning: assessing potential effects of climate change on northern spotted owl in the Pacific Northwest, USA. Biological Conservation. 143: 1432–1437.

Climate Change Impacts Group. 2004. Overview of climate change impacts in the U.S. Pacific Northwest. Seattle, WA: Western Governor's Climate Change Initiative.

Crozier, L.; Zabel, R.W.; Hamlet, A.F. 2008. Predicting differential effects of climate change at the population level with life-cycle models of spring Chinook salmon. Global Change Biology. 14: 236–249.

Daly, C.; Bachelet, D.; Lenihan, J.M.; Neilson, R.P.; Parton, W.J.; Ojima, D. 2000. Dynamic simulation of tree-grass interactions for global change studies. Ecological Applications. 10: 449–469.

Dunn, P.O.; Winkler, D.W. 1999. Climate change has affected the breeding date of tree swallows throughout North America. Proceedings of the Royal Society, London. 266: 2487–2490.

Elsner, M.M.; Cuo, L.; Vousin, N.; Deem, J.S.; Hamlet, A.F.; Vano, J.A.; Mickelson, K.E.B.; Lee, S.; Lettenmeir, D.P. 2009. Implications of 21st century climate change for the hydrology of Washington state. In: Elsner, M.M.; Littel, J.; Binder, L.W., eds. The Washington Climate Change Impacts Assessment. Seattle, WA: Center for Science in the Earth System, Joint Institute for the Study of the Atmosphere and Oceans, University of Washington: 69–106.

Finney, M.A. 2004. Landscape fire simulation and fuel treatment optimization. In: Hayes, J.L.; Ager, A.; Barbour, R.J., eds. Methods for integrated modeling of landscape change: interior Northwest landscape analysis system. Gen. Tech. Rep. PNW-GTR-610. Portland, OR: U.S. Department of Agriculture, Forest Service, Pacific Northwest Research Station: 117–131.

Folke, C. 2006. Resilience: the emergence of a perspective for social-ecological systems analyses. Global Environmental Change. 16: 253–267.

Franklin, J.F.; Hemstrom, M.A.; Van Pelt, R.; Hull, S. 2008. The case for active management of dry forest types in eastern Washington: perpetuating and creating old forest structures and functions. Olympia, WA: Washington State Department of Natural Resources. 97 p.

Franklin, J.F.; Moir, W.H.; Douglas, G.W.; Wiberg, C. 1971. Invasion of subalpine meadows by trees in the Cascade Range, Washington and Oregon. Arctic and Alpine Research. 3: 215–224.

Gaines, W.L.; Haggard, M.; Begley, J.; Lehmkuhl, J.; Lyons, A. 2010. Short-term effects of thinning and burning restoration treatments on avian community composition, density and nest survival in the eastern Cascades dry forests, Washington. Forest Science. 56(1): 88–99.

Gaines, W.L.; Lyons, A.L.; Lehmkuhl, J.F.; Haggard, M.; Begley, J.S.; Farrell, M. 2009. Chapter 8: Avian community composition, nesting ecology, and cavity-nester foraging ecology. In: Agee, J.K.; Lehmkuhl, J.F., comps. Dry forests of the northeastern Cascades Fire and Fire Surrogate Project site, Mission Creek, Okanogan-Wenatchee National Forest. Res. Pap. PNW-RP-577. Portland, OR: U.S. Department of Agriculture, Forest Service, Pacific Northwest Research Station: 108–141.

Gaines, W.L.; Haggard, M.; Lehmkuhl, J.F.; Lyons, A.L.; Harrod, R.J. 2007. Short-term response of land birds to ponderosa pine restoration. Restoration Ecology. 15(4): 670–678.

Gaines, W.L.; Lyons, A.L.; Sprague, A. 2005. Predicting the occurrence of a rare mollusk in the dry forests of north-central Washington. Northwest Science. 70(2&3): 99–105.

Gartner, S.; Reynolds, K.M.; Hessburg, P.F.; Hummel, S.; Twery, S. 2008. Decision support for evaluating landscape departure and prioritizing forest management activities in a changing environment. Forest Ecology and Management. 256: 1666–1676.

Gonzalez, P.; Nielson, R.P.; McKelvey, K.S.; Lenihan, J.M.; Drapek, R.J. 2007. Potential impacts of climate change on habitat and conservation priority areas for *Lynx canadensis* (Canada lynx). Washington, DC: U.S. Department of Agriculture, Forest Service. 19 p.

Graham, R.W.; Grimm, E.C. 1990. Effects of global climate change on the patterns of terrestrial biological communities. Trends in Ecology and Evolution. 5(9): 289–292.

Halofsky, J.E.; Peterson, D.L.; O'Halloran, K.A.; Hawkins Hoffman, C., eds. 2011. Adapting to climate change at Olympic National Forest and Olympic National Park. Gen. Tech. Rep. PNW-GTR-844. Portland, OR: U.S. Department of Agriculture, Forest Service, Pacific Northwest Research Station. 130 p.

Hamlet, A.F.; Lettenmaier, D.P. 1999. Effects of climate change on hydrology and water resources in the Columbia River basin. Journal of the American Water Resources Association. 35: 1597–1623.

Hamlet, A.F.; Mote, P.W.; Clark, M.P.; Lettenmaier, D.P. 2007. Trends in runoff, evapotranspiration, and soil moisture in the western United States. Journal of Climate. 20: 1468–1481.

Hannah, L.; Salm, R. 2004. Protected areas management in a changing climate. In: Lovejoy, T.E.; Hannah, L., eds. Climate change and biodiversity. New Haven, CT: Yale University Press. 363–374.

Harrod, R.J.; McRae, B.H.; Hartl, W.E. 1999. Historical stand reconstruction in ponderosa pine forests to guide silvicultural prescriptions. Forest Ecology and Management. 114: 433–446.

Heller, N.E.; Zavaleta, E.S. 2009. Biodiversity management in the face of climate change: a review of 22 years of recommendations. Biological Conservation. 142: 14–32.

Hessburg, P.F.; Salter, R.B.; James, K.M. 2007. Re-examining fire severity relations in pre-management era mixed conifer forests: inferences from landscape patterns of forest structure. Landscape Ecology. 22(1): 5–24.

Hessburg, P.F.; Agee, J.K.; Franklin, J.F. 2005. Dry mixed conifer forests of the inland Northwest, USA: contrasting the landscape ecology of the pre-settlement and modern eras. Forest Ecology and Management. 211: 117–139.

Hessburg, P.F.; Smith, B.G.; Salter, R.B. 1999. Detecting change in forest spatial pattern from reference condition. Ecological Applications. 9: 1232–1252.

Hessburg, P.F.; Smith, B.G.; Salter, R.B.; Kreiter, S.D. 1997. Estimating natural variation in spatial patterns of forests: a case study of the northern Cascade Mountains of Washington state. Portland, OR: U.S. Department of Agriculture, Forest Service, Pacific Northwest Research Station. 99 p.

Independent Scientific Advisory Board [ISAB]. 2007. Climate change impacts on Columbia River basin fish and wildlife. Northwest Power and Conservation Council. ISAB 2007-2. http://www.nwcouncil.org/library/isab/ISAB%20 2007-2%20Climate%20Change.pdf. (November 2007).

Intergovernmental Panel on Climate Change [IPCC]. 2007. Mitigation. Contribution of Working Group III to the 4th assessment report of the Intergovernmental Panel on Climate Change. Cambridge, United Kingdom: Cambridge University Press.

Joyce, L.A.; Blate, G.M.; Littell, J.S.; McNulty, S.G.; Millar, C.I.; Moser, S.C.; Neilson, R.P.; O'Halloran, K.; Peterson, D.L. 2008. National forests. In: Julius, S.H.; West, J.M., eds. Preliminary review of adaptation options for climate-sensitive ecosystems and resources. A report by the U.S. Climate Change Science Program and the Subcommittee on Global Change Research. Washington, DC: U.S. Environmental Protection Agency: 3-1-3-127.

Keeling, C.D.; Whorf, T.P.; Wahlen, M.; van der Plicht, J. 1995. Interannual extremes in the rate of rise of atmospheric carbon dioxide since 1980. Nature. 375: 666–670.

Kickert, R.N.; Tonella, G.; Simonov, A.; Krupa, S.V. 1999. Predictive modeling of effects under global change. Environmental Pollution. 100: 87–132.

Kiesecker, J.M.; Blaustein, A.R.; Belden, L.K. 2001. Complex causes of amphibian population declines. Nature. 410: 681–684.

Krajick, K. 2004. Climate change: All downhill from here? Science. 303: 1600–1602.

Landres, P.; Morgan, P.; Swanson, F. 1999. Overview of the use of natural variability in managing ecological systems. Ecological Applications. 9: 1279–1288.

Lawler, J.J.; Mathias, M. 2007. Climate change and the future of biodiversity in Washington. Report prepared for the Washington Biodiversity Council. College of Forest Resources. Seattle, WA: University of Washington. 42 p.

Lehmkuhl, J.F. 2004. Epiphytic lichen diversity and biomass in low-elevation forests of the eastern Washington Cascade Range, USA. Forest Ecology and Management. 187: 381–392.

Lehmkuhl, J.F.; Gould, L.; Cazares, E.; Hosford, D. 2004. Truffle abundance and mycophagy by northern flying squirrels in eastern Washington forests. Forest Ecology and Management. 200: 49–65.

Lehmkuhl, J.F.; Kistler, K.D.; Begley, J.S.; Boulanger, J. 2006. Demography of northern flying squirrels informs ecosystem management of western interior forests. Ecological Applications. 16(2): 584–600.

Lillybridge, T.R.; Kovalchik, B.L.; Williams, C.K.; Smith, B.G. 1995. Field guide for forested plant associations of the Wenatchee National Forest. Gen. Tech. Rep. PNW-GTR-359. Portland, OR: U.S. Department of Agriculture, Forest Service, Pacific Northwest Research Station. 336 p.

Littell, J.S.; Oneil, E.E.; McKenzie, D.; Hicke, J.A.; Lutz, J.A.; Norheim, R.A.; Elsner, M.M. 2009. Forest ecosystems, disturbances, and climate change in Washington state, USA. In: Elsner, M.M.; Littel, J.; Binder, L.W., eds. The Washington Climate Change Impacts Assessment. Seattle, WA: Center for Science in the Earth System, Joint Institute for the Study of the Atmosphere and Oceans, University of Washington: 255–284.

Logan, J.A.; Powell, J.A. 2001. Ghost forests, global warming, and the mountain pine beetle (Coleoptera: Scolytidae). American Entomologist. 47: 160–172.

Logan, J.A.; Regniere, J.; Powell, J.A. 2003. Assessing the impacts of global warming on forest pest dynamics. Frontiers in Ecology and Environment. 1: 130–137.

Mantua, N.; Tohver, I.; Hamlet, A. 2009. Impacts of climate change on key aspects of freshwater salmon habitat in Washington State. In: Elsner, M.M.; Littel, J.; Binder, L.W., eds. The Washington Climate Change Impacts Assessment. Seattle, WA: Center for Science in the Earth System, Joint Institute for the Study of the Atmosphere and Oceans, University of Washington: 217–254.

McKenzie, D.; Gedalof, Z.E.; Peterson, D.L.; Mote, P. 2004. Climatic change, wildfire, and conservation. Conservation Biology. 18: 890–902.

Miles, E.L.; Snover, A.K.; Hamlet, A.F.; Callahan, B.M.; Fluharty, D.L. 2000. Pacific Northwest regional assessment: the impacts of climate variability and climate change on the water resources of the Columbia River basin. Journal of the American Water Resources Association. 36: 399–420.

Millar, C. 2008. Natural resource strategies and climate change. http//www.fs.fed.us/crcc/natural-resource.shtml. (April 2009).

Millar, C.I.; Stephenson, N.L.; Stephens, S.L. 2007. Climate change and forests of the future: managing in the face of uncertainty. Ecological Applications. 17(8): 2145–2151.

Mote, P.W.; Hamlet, A.F.; Clark, M.P.; Lettenmaier, D.P. 2005. Declining mountain snowpack in western North America. Bulletin of the American Meteorlogical Society. 86: 39–49.

Mote, P. 2003a. Trends in snow water equivalent in the Pacific Northwest and their climatic causes. Geophysical Research Letters. 30: 1601–1604.

Mote, P. 2003b. Trends in temperature and precipitation in the Pacific Northwest during the twentieth century. Northwest Science. 77: 271–282.

Mote, P.W.; Canning, D.J.; Fluharty, D.L. 1999. Impacts of climate variability and change, Pacific Northwest. Seattle, WA: National Atmospheric and Oceanic Administration, Office of Global Programs.

Nakawatase, J.M.; Peterson, D.L. 2006. Spatial variability in forest growth—climate relationships in the Olympic Mountains, Washington. Canadian Journal of Forest Research. 36: 77–91.

Neilson, R.P.; Drapek, R.J. 1998. Potentially complex biosphere responses to transient global warming. Global Change Biology. 4: 505–521.

Neilson, R.P.; Pitelka, L.F.; Solomon, A.M.; Nathan, R.; Midgley, G.F.; Fragoso, J.M.; Lischke, H.; Thompson, K. 2005. Forecasting regional to global plant migration in response to climate change. BioScience. 55: 749–759.

O'Brien, K.; Hayward, B.; Berkes, F. 2009. Rethinking social contracts: building resilience in a changing climate. Ecology and Society. 14(2): 12.

Ogden, A.E.; Innes, J.L. 2009. Application of structured decision making to an assessment of climate change vulnerabilities and adaption options for sustainable forest management. Ecology and Society. 14(1): 11.

Opdam, P.; Wascher, D. 2004. Climate change meets habitat fragmentation: linking landscape and biogeographical scale levels in research and conservation. Biological Conservation. 117: 285.

Parmesan, C. 2006. Ecological and evolutionary responses to recent climate change. Annual Review of Ecology, Evolution, and Systematics. 37: 637–669.

Pearcy, W.G. 1997. Salmon production in changing ocean domains. In: Stouder, D.J.; Bisson, P.A.; Naiman, R.J., eds. Pacific salmon and their ecosystems: status and future options. New York: Chapman and Hall: 331–352.

Pearsons, T.N.; Li, H.W.; Lamberti, G.A. 1992. Influence of habitat complexity on resistance to flooding and resilience of stream fish assemblages. Transactions of the American Fisheries Society. 121: 427–436.

Perry, D.A.; Hessburg, P.F.; Skinner, C.N.; Spies, T.A.; Stephens, S.L.; Henry Taylor, A.; Franklin, J.F.; McComb, B.; Riegel, G. 2011. The ecology of mixed severity fire regimes in Washington, Oregon, and northern California. Forest Ecology and Management. 262: 703–717.

Peterson, D.L.; Millar, C.I.; Joyce, L.A.; Furniss, M.J.; Halofsky, J.E.; Neilson, R.P.; Morelli, T.L. 2011a. Responding to climate change in national forests: a guidebook for developing adaptation options. Gen. Tech. Rep. PNW-GTR-855. Portland, OR: U.S. Department of Agriculture, Forest Service, Pacific Northwest Research Station. 109 p.

Peterson, D.L.; Halofsky, J.E.; Johnson, M.C. 2011b. Chapter 10: Managing and adapting to changing fire regimes in a warmer climate. In: McKenzie, D.; Miller, C.; Falk, D.A., eds. The landscape ecology of fire. Ecological Studies 213, Springer Science and Business Media, New York: 249–267.

Peterson, D.W.; Peterson, D.L. 1994. Effects of climate on radial growth of subalpine conifers in the North Cascade Mountains. Canadian Journal of Forest Research. 24: 1921–1932.

Peterson, D.; Peterson, D. 2001. Mountain hemlock growth responds to climatic variability at annual and decadal time scales. Ecology. 82: 3330–3345.

Peterson, D.W.; Peterson, D.L.; Ettl, G.J. 2002. Growth responses of subalpine fir to climatic variability in the Pacific Northwest. Canadian Journal of Forest Research. 32: 1503–1517.

Price, J.T. 2002. Global warming and songbirds: Washington. The birdwatcher's guide to global warming. www.abcbirds.org/climatechange. (April 2008).

Reeves, G.H.; Everest, F.H.; Hall, J.D. 1987. Interactions between the redside shiner (*Richardsonius balteatus*) and the steelhead trout (*Salmo gairdneri*) in western Oregon: the influence of water temperature. Canadian Journal of Fisheries and Aquatic Sciences. 44: 1602–1613.

Root, T.L. 1992. Temperature mediated range changes in wintering passerine birds. Bulletin of the Ecological Society of America. 73: 327.

Root, T.L. 1993. Effects of global climate change on North American birds and their communities. In: Kareiva, P.M.; Kingsolver, J.G.; Huey, R.B., eds. Biotic interactions and global change. Sunderland, MA: Sinauer Associates, Inc.: 280–292.

Root, T.L.; Price, J.T.; Hall, K.R.; Schneider, S.H.; Rosenzweig, C.; Pounds, J.A. 2003. Fingerprints of global warming on wild animals and plants. Nature. 421: 57–60.

Sanderson, B.L.; Barnas, K.A.; Wargo Rub, M.A. 2009. Nonindigenous species of the Pacific Northwest: an overlooked risk to endangered salmon? Bioscience. 59(3): 245–256.

Seppala, R.; Buck, A.; Katila, P. 2009. Adaptation of forests and people to climate change: a global assessment report. IUFRO World Series, Volume 22. Helsinki, Finland: International Union of Forest Research Organizations: 135–186.

Singleton, P.H.; Lehmkuhl, J.F.; Gaines, W.L.; Graham, S. 2010. Barred owl space use and habitat selection in the eastern Cascades, Washington: implications for northern spotted owl conservation. Journal of Wildlife Management. 74(2): 285–294.

Snover, A.K.; Hamlet, A.F.; Lettenmaier, D.P. 2003. Climate-change scenarios for water planning studies: pilot applications in the Pacific Northwest. Bulletin of the American Meteorological Society. 84: 1513–1518.

Spies, T.A.; Hemstrom, M.A.; Youngblood, A.; Hummel, S. 2006. Conserving old growth forest diversity in disturbance-prone landscapes. Conservation Biology. 20: 351–362.

Spies, T.A.; Giesen, T.W.; Swanson, F.J.; Franklin, J.F.; Lach, D.; Johnson, K.N. 2010. Climate change adaptation strategies for federal forests of the Pacific Northwest, USA: ecological, policy, and socio-economic perspectives. Landscape Ecology. 25(8): 1185–1199.

Stewart, I.T.; Cayan, D.R.; Dettinger, M.D. 2004. Changes in snowmelt runoff timing in western North America under a 'business as usual' climate change scenario. Climate Change. 62: 217–232.

Thomas, C.D.; Lennon, J.J. 1999. Birds extend their ranges northward. Nature. 399: 213.

Thomas, C.D.; Cameron, A.; Green, R.E.; Green, R.E.; Bakkenes, M.; Beaumont, L.J.; Collingham, Y.C.; Erasmus, B.F.N.; de Siqueira, M.F.; Grainger, A.; Hannah, L.; Hughes, L.; Huntley, B.F.; van Jaarsveld, A.S.; Midgley, G.F.; Miles, L.; Ortega-Huerta, M.A.; Peterson, A.T.; Phillips, O.L.; Williams, S.E. 2004. Extinction risk from climate change. Nature. 427: 145–148.

Turner, B.L.; Kasperson, R.E.; Matson, P.A.; McCarthy, J.J.; Corell, R.W.; Christensen, L.; Eckley, N.; Kasperson, J.X.; Luers, A.; Martello, M.L.; Polsky, C.; Pulsipher, A.; Schiller, A. 2003. A framework for vulnerability analysis in sustainability science. Proceedings of the National Academy of Sciences. 100(14): 8074–8079.

U.S. Department of Agriculture [USDA]. 2010. Strategic Plan: FY 2010–2015. Washington, DC. 33 p.

U.S. Department of Agriculture, Forest Service [USDA FS]. 1997. Forest-wide assessments for late-successional reserves and managed late-successional areas, Wenatchee National Forest. Wenatchee, WA: Okanogan-Wenatchee National Forest. 217 p.

U.S. Department of Agriculture, Forest Service [USDA FS]. 1998a. Eastside screens: interim direction for the management of national forest lands within the Pacific Northwest Region. Portland, OR: Pacific Northwest Region.

U.S. Department of Agriculture, Forest Service [USDA FS]. 1998b. Forest-wide assessments for late-successional reserves and managed late-successional areas, Okanogan National Forest. Wenatchee, WA: Okanogan-Wenatchee National Forest.

U.S. Department of Agriculture, Forest Service [USDA FS]. 2008a. Strategic framework for responding to climate change. Washington, DC.

U.S. Department of Agriculture, Forest Service [USDA FS]. 2008b. Climate change considerations in project level NEPA analysis. Washington, DC.

U.S. Department of Agriculture, Forest Service [USDA FS]. 2010. National roadmap for responding to climate change. Washington, DC. 30 p.

U.S. Department of Agriculture [USDA]; U.S. Department of the Interior [USDI]. 1994. Record of decision for amendments to Forest Service and Bureau of Land Management planning documents within the range of the northern spotted owl. Portland, OR: U.S. Department of Agriculture, Forest Service and U.S. Department of Interior, Bureau of Land Management.

Vano, J.A.; Scott, M.; Voisin, N.; Stockle, C.O.; Hamlet, A.F.; Mickelson, K.E.B.; Elsner, M.M.; Lettenmaier, D.P. 2009. Climate change impacts on water management and irrigated agriculture in the Yakima River basin, Washington, USA. In: Elsner, M.M.; Littel, J.; Binder, L.W., eds. The Washington Climate Change Impacts Assessment. Seattle, WA: Center for Science in the Earth System, University of Washington.

Weaver, K.; Morales, V.; Sprague, A.G.; Gaines, B.; Aubry, C. 2009. Biogeographic and taxonomic analysis of the Chelan Mountainsnail, Okanogan-Wenatchee National Forest, Washington. Wenatchee, WA: U.S. Department of Agriculture, Forest Service.

Westerling, A.L.; Hidalgo, H.G.; Cayan, D.R.; Swetnam, T.W. 2006. Warming and earlier spring increase western U.S. forest wildfire activity. Science. 313: 940–943.

Williams, C.K.; Lillybridge, T.R. 1983. Forested plant associations of the Okanogan National Forest. R6-Ecol-132b-1983. Portland, OR: U.S. Department of Agriculture, Forest Service, Pacific Northwest Region. 140 p.

Woodsmith, R. 2008. Climate Change Implications for Aquatics: snow and stream hydrology. Wenatchee, WA: U.S. Department of Agriculture, Forest Service, Pacific Northwest Region.

Woodward, A.; Schreiner, E.G.; Silsbee, D.G. 1995. Climate, geography, and tree establishment in subalpine meadows of the Olympic Mountains, Washington, USA. Arctic and Alpine Research. 27: 217–225.

Wormworth, J.; Mallon, K. 2006. Bird species and climate change. Sydney, Australia. World Wildlife Fund. 12 p.

Wotton, B.M.; Flannigan, M.D. 1993. Length of the fire season in a changing climate. Forestry Chronicle. 69: 187–192.